TEMPLES

A Photographic Journey of Temples, Lands, and People

DON BUSATH

EUROPEAN HISTORY CONSULTANT AND CONTRIBUTIONS BY
MATTHEW HEISS

DESERET
BOOK

SALT LAKE CITY, UTAH

Library of Congress Cataloging-in-Publication Data

Busath, Don.
 Temples : a photographic journey of temples, lands, and people / Don
Busath.
     p. cm.
  Includes index.
  ISBN 1-59038-346-X (hardbound : alk. paper)
  1. Mormon temples—Pictorial works. I. Title.
  BX8643.T4B87 2004
  246'.9589332—dc22
                              2004011231

Manufactured in China
R.R. Donnelley and Sons, Schenzen, China

10   9   8   7   6   5   4   3   2   1

18961

Art Direction: Richard Erickson

CONTENTS

Contents

This book on temples of The Church of Jesus Christ of Latter-day Saints has been both a greater privilege and much more work than I initially anticipated. When I first envisioned the idea in 2001, my thought was to create a photographic book of the temples connected to important Church history sites. My wife, Donna, and I embarked on a trip to St. George, Utah, to produce a prototype to see if there was an interest in such a book. But even before submitting the idea to the publisher, I had a sense that the historical aspects of latter-day temples had been very well covered and that maybe current photos were not the ideal way to deal with history.

The pictorial layout of our prototype had merit and was satisfying to me, but the publisher's reaction supported my own wonderings. My contacts at Deseret Book suggested that a pictorial presentation of the temples along with their *cultural surroundings* might be more appealing for the reader. That set the stage for the concept of this book; it also created the necessity for a much larger book! The idea of temples being *in* the world but not *of* the world came to me as I looked at the image of the Las Vegas Nevada Temple juxtaposed against the lights of the downtown strip in the background.

As I developed the concept further, I decided to use three categories of illustrative photography in this collection: *architectural,* *pictorial,* and *street photography.* By combining all three, I was able to more fully convey a feeling and understanding about our latter-day temples and their settings around the world.

BACKGROUND IN ARCHITECTURAL PHOTOGRAPHY

I received my training in architectural work from Hal Rumel. He was my mentor and employer for fifteen years. He had been an apprentice to a Salt Lake commercial photographer named Davis, then studied at the Art Center in Los Angeles. Later Hal became the chief photographer for the Lockheed Corporation.

Hal equipped me with an 8x10-inch view camera, along with the admonition that anything smaller was not adequate for professional architecture work. Hal passed away in 1975, and he may be very unhappy with me if he is aware, on the other side of the veil, that since I sold my studio to my son Drake I began to use 35-mm cameras exclusively.

FILM

Why was Hal correct about the large-format view camera? When I started working with him in 1959, most commercial work was still done in black and white, and the highest quality photographs of buildings required perspective correction and contact print detail—both of which required a larger image. In addition, many of the government contracts we photographed for insisted on a larger negative.

With that background, why can I feel justified now in using 35-mm equipment? In the 1970s, I learned about and purchased two perspective-correction lenses from Nikon. That was a breakthrough for me because I discovered I enjoyed the small equipment. I didn't sell my view cameras until the late 1980s, however—they were sort of a security blanket!

Another development that made small film more feasible was the introduction to the market of Velvia film, manufactured by the Fuji Company. Kodak's Kodachrome film had been the standard for years (even used by *National Geographic*), giving excellent grain structure and sharpness. But the photographer had to send exposed film to Kodak for processing, and for many applications it needed

Las Vegas Nevada Temple.

Foliage from the grounds of the Laie Hawaii Temple.

filtration because of excess cyan. The new Velvia film had better-than-life renditions of the greens, and it could be processed in E-6 chemistry, which meant fast turn-around time in most professional labs. Velvia film gave near instant gratification—which is completely expected in the new digital age!

DIGITAL IMAGING

Nikon cameras had been my choice since photojournalists had used them during the Korean War. My first Nikon was an S2 range finder type, which was later replaced by the single-lens-reflex F series. As updates came along, I eventually purchased the F4 and F5. Then, two years ago, I acquired the Nikon D1X digital. This was a logical transfer, since those three cameras all use the same lenses and accessories. To maintain the highest quality for this book, I have used film as the main capture, with digital backup.

As I progressed through the process of creating this book, I have come to realize that digital imaging has some definite advantages over film. Perhaps the most obvious advantage is the immediate feedback digital imaging gives you, telling you whether or not the exposure is in the ballpark. I often work in the margins of light for mood and expression. Light levels are often very low, requiring long exposures, and when buildings are lighted at dusk and dawn I might want to try an exposure that the light meter may not adequately evaluate. In such cases, personal judgment quickly comes into play. Working with positive film, this subtle control of the image can be achieved only by "bracketing" the exposure in 1/3 stops,

which the Nikon professional system provides. But sometimes during the course of a bracket, the light pattern or intensity might change several times! Digital imaging helps to overcome this problem.

Besides refining work with exposure levels, an instant digital check can verify decisions about composition, framing, and content; when human figures are included in the photograph, a digital camera can help assess their gestures and the sharpness of the exposure.

For the air-traveling photographer, one great advantage of a digital camera is that the X-ray equipment used for security won't fog the images, as can happen with film if great pains are not taken to safeguard against it. (When I do carry film, I use the following safeguards: I always carry my film with me personally, never in my luggage, and I use very, very slow film, 50 ISO or slower.)

OTHER EQUIPMENT

Besides the Nikon cameras and perspective-correcting lenses I have already mentioned, I also use several other essential items of equipment. Fifty-plus years have convinced me that a sturdy, high-quality tripod is a necessity! To make the tripod effective, I also use a cable release or electronic release. For a tripod used when traveling, one needs to steer a fine line between weight, practical adjustments for a low and high camera platform, and folding capabilities to fit tight travel situations in cars and other conveyances (rowboats, feluccas, horses, buses, trains, gondolas, trams, and so forth). The minimum weight to support my camera and steady my long lenses is 6.5 pounds. The legs are a carbon alloy, which saves on the weight. The high-quality head weighs as much as the legs. Extended, my tripod holds the camera at 6.5 feet, which helps me look over some hedges, fences, and walls; folded, it is only 32 inches long.

Another good camera support is a beanbag, which I can use on the ground, in car windows, and on other existing perches.

If you hope to come back with the photographs you've taken, you also need an extra camera body. Once I arrived in Cairo, Egypt, for a three-week assignment. When I exposed the first film on my Hasselblad camera, the camera locked up. I was grateful to have two backup camera bodies with me.

For this temple book, I carried lenses for my Nikons (from

Harbor scene on Africa's Gold Coast near the Elmina Castle.

14 mm to 400 mm) with me. In most cases I had never seen these locations before, except in photos or renderings, and I wasn't certain what I'd need. Although my Nikons have excellent metering systems, I felt the need to carry an incident light meter, a reflected light 1-degree spot meter, and a color temperature meter. I also packed a few essential tools for the camera and the tripod, with lens and sensor cleaning materials in the bag, and I was always careful to take the instruction manuals for *all* the above equipment!

WHY THIS BOOK WAS CREATED

It is my hope that through this book members of the Church will enjoy a pleasant recognition of the rich diversity of the temples that now dot the earth. I hope that the images presented here will give the reader a sense that the Church is indeed a worldwide family. As you leaf through these pages and see many styles of building and design, with samplings of the communities they represent, I hope you can feel the warmth of those communities. I also hope that you can take great comfort in the fact that in every temple, large or small, the same blessings are available to every person who qualifies to enter the House of the Lord.

As I have worked to edit and present the temple photographs, I usually have music playing; in some ways the images in this book are "music for the eye," more to enjoy than to study. My wish was to sequence them to flow according to their color and style. To a degree the order is chronological, but even more importantly, I sought to continually refresh the eye as the photographs take us from historical to modern, from urban to rural. Many of the photographs have identifying captions, but some do not. A number of the pictures that were taken at the temple or in the surrounding areas simply speak for themselves and need no written comment.

Naturally, every photographer hopes that people will enjoy the colors, form, composition, and lighting that provoked him to snap the shutter. My greatest hope, though, is that each member of the Church will feel what I have come to feel—a sort of ownership and especially a membership in the great worldwide family of The Church of Jesus Christ of Latter-day Saints.

In these days of serious attacks on the family, we have a wonderful assurance that our Heavenly Father loves and cares about each of our families—and each of us as individuals: the ever-increasing availability to every member of the eternal blessings of the temple.

ACKNOWLEDGMENTS

I would like to express my thanks to close associates who have patiently listened to my explanations for the last two years about being retired from my portrait photography, and who then have listened to the unending details of this temple book project. I hope they are still my friends!

Even more important, I thank my wife, Donna, who devoted her great mental abilities, her engaging personality, and her calmness through hundreds of phone calls, emails, and mailings to work out the unending details of our travels. She also contributed her physical presence through all these trips and agreed to expend a grand share of our savings!

Jana Erickson of Deseret Book has been an advocate of the project ideas I come up with, and the conduit of information, encouragement, and ideas to advance the cause. I appreciate her experience, good sense, and good taste that have helped in my desire to share my images with people who care deeply about the subject.

We were able to utilize the very specialized talents and knowledge of Church historian Matthew Heiss. He is a good friend and fellow ward member, and was a necessary facilitator on the European part of our journey. His connections in Germany, Switzerland, England, and the Netherlands—coupled with his ability to negotiate the roads and languages and to make many arrangements for our lodging and transportation—were vital to our success on this adventure.

The Swiss Alps tower over a field in Bern, Switzerland.

Matthew Heiss made special arrangements with acquaintances to shepherd us in the Preston, England, area. Our very kind hosts were John and Chris Fell. We will always remember their contribution to our lovely memories of England. In Berlin, we were the overnight guests of the Nipko family, who drove us in their van to historic sites in West and East Berlin. They lived in West Berlin and were very grateful for the allied airlift that sustained them through the Cold War years. I had been a child during the Second World War, so I was very moved at seeing remnants of Hitler Germany, such as the Olympic Stadium, the Brandenburg Gate, the Berlin Wall, and Checkpoint Charlie. I had chills as I remembered those dark days. Klaus and Helga Nipko were very thoughtful and kind to us, and the insight they provided into Germany's history will remain part of my personal understanding. Matthew Heiss was also responsible for gathering and writing most of the historical captions in the Europe area.

Every single temple president and temple recorder was more than gracious in contributing insightful information at every temple, and they often went out of their way to make us welcome, comfortable, and cared for while we were in their area.

Our dear friends Doug and Ruth McEwan were our Mexico connection. They first shared a trip with us to the Mexico City area in the 1980s. Ruth has directed tours there, and she has a great passion and respect for Mexico and its people. Doug is a fellow photographer. We were thrilled when they accepted our invitation to accompany us to the Ciudad Juárez and Colonial Juárez temples, across the border from El Paso, Texas. Their help and friendship were most important and were deeply appreciated.

I believe that all of our five children and twenty-seven grandchildren in some way had a connection to this book, because we combined our photography schedule with family reunions, weddings, missionaries serving, and get-togethers on both coasts and in South America. We were able to attend church with our missionary granddaughter, Lorna Castleton, in Rio de Janeiro—a short jet hop from Campinas, Brazil. On the East coast, our musician grandson, Gavin, was able to drive from his home in Rhode Island and meet us at the Boston temple.

Our photographer son, Drake Busath, made a special and fortuitous addition to this book. While the book was in process, he was

Spires of the San Diego California Temple.

engaged to speak to the professional photographers of South Korea on the art of portrait photography and the new digital age. (He was particularly agreeable to accept this request because his son Bromley was just finishing his mission in South Korea.) When we heard of this assignment, I asked Drake if he could record some images of the Seoul Korea Temple and the Tokyo Japan Temple, along with their surroundings. He agreed, and his contribution is a wonderful addition to this book.

Photographer Deanne Parry, our daughter, is the steward of my pictorial files and has been a mentor and guide into the world of digital-imaging control.

We acknowledge our debt to Chad S. Hawkins for *The First 100 Temples* (Deseret Book, 2001), and to Elder John K. Carmack, who provided references to temples from the Old Testament. They were both invaluable sources of reference and research during our preparation of these materials.

Besides those mentioned, Donna and I acknowledge many more people in our hearts. Above all, we recognize heavenly guidance and constant influence through this entire effort. Many small miracles of weather, safety, and inspiration constantly nourished our effort, and for that we are profoundly thankful.

One thing have I desired of the Lord, that will I seek after; that I may dwell in the house of the Lord all the days of my life, to behold the beauty of the Lord, and to enquire in his temple.
—PSALM 27:4

DEDICATED 1846
REBUILT AND REDEDICATED 2002

When we first visited Nauvoo in 1970 with our young family, the city contained only a few historical Latter-day Saint buildings and no more than a depression in the ground where the temple had been. What a change had occurred by the time we revisited Nauvoo in 2002 to see the new temple! Historic in Nauvoo included many restored houses and shops and, of course, a magnificent functioning temple. The beauty of the temple and its surroundings was breathtaking. It is still hard for me to fathom how the original structure was raised by the Saints.

Joseph Smith store.

Heber C. Kimball home.

Sunstones and window details.

*In my distress I called upon the Lord, and cried unto
my God: he heard my voice out of his temple.*
—PSALM 18:6

Sarah Granger Kimball home.

Kitchen detail from Brigham Young home.

A flock of geese on a nearby pond.

ABOVE: "David's Chambers," a favored spot of David Smith, son of Joseph.
RIGHT: Original bridge over drainage stream in Nauvoo.

Well at Brigham Young home.

ABOVE: *Young performers at Nauvoo visitors' center.*
BELOW: *Joseph Smith "Mansion House," used by Joseph as home and hotel.*

Above: *Kitchen at Brigham Young home.*
Left: *Temple tower close-up.*

Graves of Joseph Smith Sr. and Lucy Mack Smith.

Jonathan Browning home and gun shop.

Blue heron, Mississippi River.

View of temple across Mississippi River.

ABOVE: *Baby sparrows in nest.*
RIGHT: *Temple from southeast.*

DEDICATED 1877

The exquisite whiteness of the St. George Utah Temple contrasts with the earthy red rock of the valley and the surrounding mesas. Brigham Young selected the site against the advice of builders.

The marshy area required much preparation, with lava rock being used for the footings and foundations. Brigham also pressed for a higher tower for the temple, which he felt was "squatty." Several months after his death, the short tower was destroyed by lightning. The builders replaced it with the higher tower they knew Brigham wanted. As a result of the placement and design of the temple, it dominates the city from all directions, including the freeway that runs nearby. It is indeed the hub of the wheel of activity in St. George, Utah.

The St. George valley ringed by the bluffs and mesas of the area.

The territorial statehouse in Fillmore to the north.

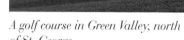

A golf course in Green Valley, north of St. George.

ABOVE: *Birds settle on the lovely clock tower that tops the venerable St. George Tabernacle. Several blocks from the temple, the tabernacle served as an important meeting place for early Saints.*

ABOVE: *Zion National Park, located a few miles to the northeast.*
ABOVE RIGHT: *Brigham Young's St. George home.*
BELOW: *The temple visitors' center, with the temple towering behind.*

ABOVE: *Pine Valley, to the north of St. George.*
BELOW: *Las Vegas, southwest of St. George.*

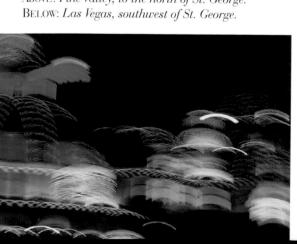

And it shall come to pass in the last days, that the mountain of the Lord's house shall be established in the top of the mountains, and shall be exalted above the hills; and all nations shall flow unto it. And many people shall go and say, Come ye, and let us go up to the mountain of the Lord, to the house of the God of Jacob; and he will teach us of his ways, and we will walk in his paths: for out of Zion shall go forth the law, and the word of the Lord from Jerusalem.

—ISAIAH 2:2–3

DEDICATED 1893

The sesquicentennial wagon train working its way down East Canyon is, to me, an appropriate companion to this new view of the Salt Lake Temple. Several days after arriving in the valley in such a wagon train, Brigham Young and a small group walked to a spot between two forks of City Creek and declared, "Here we will build a temple to our God." My wife, Donna, and I believe we had ancestors in that small group.

This temple, standing at the very focal point of Salt Lake City, has rightly become the most prominent symbol of The Church of Jesus Christ of Latter-day Saints throughout the world.

A view of the Main Street Plaza and Conference Center from the Joseph Smith Memorial Building.

ABOVE: *LDS Conference Center.*
BELOW: *Close-up view of Conference Center.*

Main Street Plaza dressed for Christmas.

LEFT: *Olympic awards plaza. Note the giant images on the high-rise buildings in downtown Salt Lake City.*
BELOW: *Interior of the Conference Center during general conference.*

Spires and towers of downtown Salt Lake City.

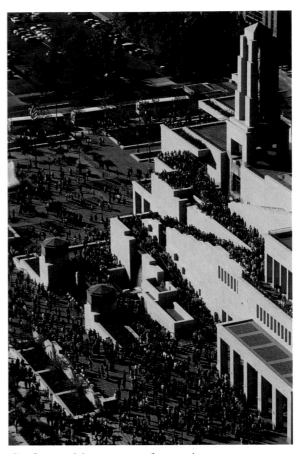

Conference visitors emerge after meeting.

ABOVE AND RIGHT: *Wasatch Mountains and the "greatest snow on earth."*

OGDEN UTAH TEMPLE

DEDICATED 1972

The Ogden Utah Temple was the first temple to be built in Utah since the completion of the Salt Lake Temple in 1893. Ogden is home to a major rail hub and is a close neighbor to the United States Air Force's Hill Field. Ogden shares the mountains and other attributes of Salt Lake City, her sister city to the south, and was host to major Olympic ski events at Snow Park to the east of the city.

A ski area located on the northern part of the Wasatch Mountains, near Ogden.

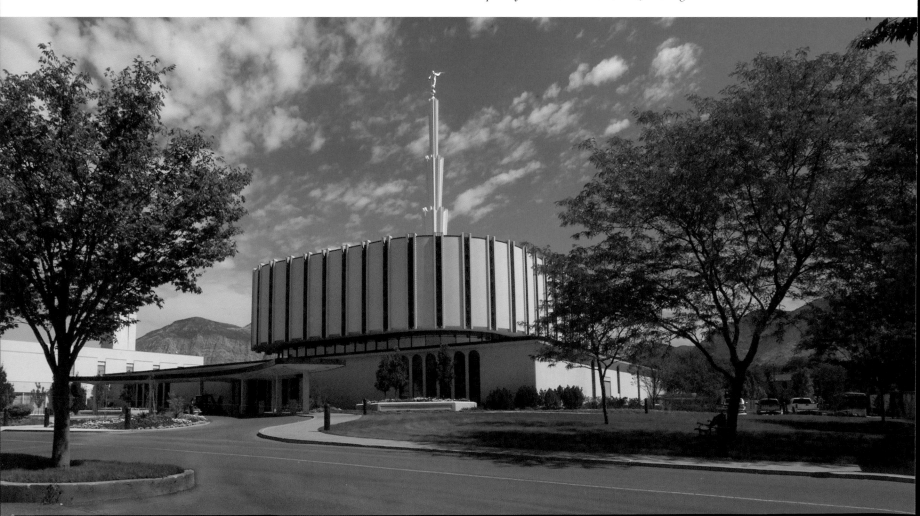

DEDICATED 1919

The first temple to be dedicated after the Salt Lake Temple, this edifice occupies a natural place in a paradise one-half mile from the beach. The groundbreaking for this temple was done by President Joseph F. Smith, who had served as a missionary in Hawaii many decades earlier. Unfortunately, President Smith died in 1918 and therefore did not survive to see the completion of this beautiful temple.

BELOW: *The view from the temple entrance to the ocean.*

ABOVE AND BELOW: *Typical scenes from beautiful Hawaii.*

ABOVE: *Fountains on the temple grounds.* BELOW: *The skyline of Honolulu, Hawaii.*

DEDICATED 1888

The site for the third temple to be completed in Utah was dedicated by Brigham Young in 1877, only months before he died. Manti is in the very center of the state of Utah, and its temple has served great multitudes from the many communities in that part of the state. The turkey industry is an important part of the agricultural base of the community.

An annual "Mormon Miracle Pageant" takes place here on Temple Hill which draws crowds of 20,000 for each performance.

The Manti–La Sal Mountains, which are wonderful for recreation, also provide grazing for cattle and sheep, giving a beautiful display of scenes like this on the Skyline Drive.

Typical winter fog shrouds the historic Logan Tabernacle, located a few blocks from the temple.

DEDICATED 1884

The city of Logan occupies a large alpine valley north of Brigham City, Utah, and is the home of Utah State University. This historic temple, dedicated by John Taylor, has made major contributions to the spiritual strength of the area. It serves large areas in northern Utah, southwestern Wyoming, and southeastern Idaho. Many leaders in the Church trace their roots to this temple area.

MEXICO CITY MEXICO TEMPLE

DEDICATED 1983

I had two impressions when I traveled to Mexico City and the surrounding area: warmth and color. The people are generally warm and friendly, and the use of bright color in buildings and displays is natural and charming.

The temple fits the motif of ancient Mayan structures and has been a blessing to the growth of the Church throughout this region. This temple, which is one of twelve in Mexico (either in operation or planned), serves more than 300,000 members of the Church from 128 stakes.

ABOVE: *A traditional folklórico performance.*
BELOW: *A modern shopping center in Mexico City.*

ABOVE AND BELOW: *The architecture of the Mexico City Mexico Temple reflects that of typical Mayan ruins found at Teotenango, Mexico.*

Brick making in the area of Cholula.

Santuario de Guadalupe.

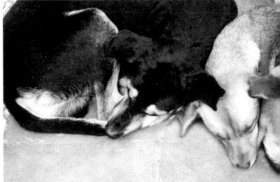

ABOVE: *Sleeping dogs.*
LEFT: *Goat herding near Puebla.*

ABOVE: *Girl descending stairs.*
BELOW: *Street market in Taxco.*

ABOVE: *Ladies of San Angel near the home of Diego Rivera, a famous Mexican artist.* BELOW: *Farming community; Toluca, Mexico.*

DEDICATED 1923

The long road trip from Salt Lake City north to Canada—through sparsely populated areas of farmland, sagebrush, prairies, beautiful lakes, and great mountains—provided me with a profound gratitude for the small group of Saints that traveled the long distance from Utah to establish the community of Cardston in the 1880s.

The temple stands solid and bold in this agricultural area. Inside the temple we were rewarded with a richness of woods and a decorating and painting approach that were unique to my experience up to that time. The architecture, inside and out, fits the eternal purpose of this temple.

The Cardston Alberta Temple was the first temple built outside the United States. (The Laie Hawaii Temple, which was dedicated four years earlier, was built in a United States territory.)

Holiness becometh thine house, O Lord.
—PSALM 93:5

ABOVE AND BELOW: *A beautiful wilderness lies a short distance from the city of Cardston.*

BERN SWITZERLAND TEMPLE

DEDICATED 1955

This is a temple of historic firsts. It was the first temple built in Europe, the first temple to use modern audiovisual equipment to present sacred ordinances, and the first temple to make ordinances available in many different languages (currently 17). The setting is certainly among the most elegant and beautiful the earth has to offer.

ABOVE: *The temple is the background for the ward meetinghouse as the Saints gather on a beautiful Sunday morning.*
BELOW: *A neighborhood in the city of Zurich.*

ABOVE: *Farm fields and forest near Bern.*
BELOW: *In the distance are the spectacular Swiss Alps, including the legendary Eiger Mountain.*

Hikers in the mountains near Grindelwald.

DEDICATED 1956

From the roadway, the Los Angeles California Temple seems deceptively normal in scale and size. When one comes closer, however, the massive scale of the building begins to become apparent. For instance, the spire tower is very impressive; at 257 feet, it rises 40 feet higher than the highest spire on the Salt Lake Temple. (For a sense of scale, note the people near the entrance in the photograph to the left.) At the time of its construction, the Los Angeles California Temple was the largest in the Church.

Although plans to construct this temple were announced in the 1930s, because of World War II work did not actually begin until 1951.

ABOVE: *Temple entrance at dusk.*
BELOW: *Lovely landscaping surrounds the temple.*

ABOVE: *Beautiful ponds grace the side of the temple.*
BELOW: *The Manor House has a history dating back to Elizabethan times; it has served a variety of purposes for temple leadership, patrons, and full-time missionaries.*

ABOVE: *A scene in the British countryside.*
RIGHT: *Statue of Richard the Lion-Hearted,*
outside the Houses of Parliament in London.

OAKLAND CALIFORNIA TEMPLE

DEDICATED 1964

The Oakland California Temple commands a view of the cities of Oakland and San Francisco. In 1924, Elder George Albert Smith, a member of the Quorum of the Twelve, was visiting the San Francisco Bay area. He had been speaking with a local Church leader, W. Aird MacDonald, on the roof terrace of the Fremont Hotel. The sunset was setting the Oakland hills ablaze, lighting it with a golden glow. Elder Smith was quiet for a time, gazing intently at the hill. Then he said, "Brother MacDonald, I can almost see in a vision a white temple of the Lord high upon those hills, an ensign to all world travelers as they come through the Golden Gate into this wonderful harbor."

The lighted temple can indeed be seen throughout the area; it has even been used to orient airline pilots coming to this destination.

BELOW: *View of Oakland in the foreground and San Francisco in the background. Notice the temple spire catching the morning light at left of photo.*

ABOVE: *Close-up view of sculptured panel on the north side of the temple showing Christ with his disciples in Jerusalem.* BELOW: *The Golden Gate Bridge in the fog.*

SEATTLE WASHINGTON TEMPLE

DEDICATED 1980

This very high walled temple uses a design of stalks of wheat as its motif on the front façade. The temple is placed on a wooded hill with an abundance of gardens, walkways, and decorative pools and fountains.

The Church has seen phenomenal growth in the state of Washington in the last few decades. In 1960 there were only 11,000 members of the Church in the state. Now there are nearly a quarter of a million members in fifty-three stakes—and three temples.

Mt. Hood as seen from the air.

For a day in thy courts is better than a thousand [elsewhere].
I had rather be a doorkeeper in the house of my God,
than to dwell in the tents of wickedness.

—PSALM 84:10

DEDICATED 2001

The location of this temple has great significance in Church history. It was in this area that the Saints stopped for the winter (and sometimes longer) as they made their way west from Nauvoo. In the nearby cemetery are buried approximately 600 Saints who died at Winter Quarters from illness, hunger, and exposure. For a time, Winter Quarters was the headquarters of the Church.

Visitors' Center.

Historic Florence mill.

Cattle taking a cooling dip.

Pioneer cabin at Mt. Pisgah, on the Mormon Trail in Iowa.

Broad horizon from an Iowa state highway.

ABOVE: *Road scene near Mt. Pisgah.* BELOW: *Detail of temple door.*

DEDICATED 1997

Missouri is a very important place to The Church of Jesus Christ of Latter-day Saints. Independence, Missouri, is the prophesied location of the great temple of the New Jerusalem, and Adam-ondi-Ahman has both historical and future significance. About 170 years before the dedication of the St. Louis Missouri Temple, the governor of Missouri ordered the extermination of all Mormons living in the state.

Now the Church has returned, and a temple of peace has been erected. The St. Louis Missouri Temple was the fiftieth temple in operation in the Church.

During the temple dedication, President Thomas S. Monson commented on the Spirit of St. Louis, shown here in replica. He said, "The temple brought a new Spirit of St. Louis." The original airplane hangs in the Smithsonian.

ABOVE: *The famous St. Louis Gateway Arch speaks of the strength of middle America.*
BELOW: *The interior of the Community of Christ temple, with its spiral shape.*

The Liberty Jail reminds us of the great difficulty and sacrifice of the early Saints. A full-sized replica of the jail is found in the visitors' center.

DEDICATED 1989

My wife and I feel a special emotional connection to the Portland Oregon Temple. We first came here to attend an endowment session of a granddaughter before her mission, and then we later returned to attend her wedding. The first trip was rainy and hurried, and I had only vague impressions of the outside of the building, although I remembered the delicate shape. The next trip I came prepared to photograph the building and grounds, and we were able to spend several wonderful days here.

The temple is set in a heavily wooded area, first purchased by the Church as a possible location for a junior college.

The temple's atrium is a lovely, light-infused garden with glass and marble. Because of the high incidence of rain, wedding and family groups are allowed to come inside for photographs without recommends if proper standards are kept.

Beautifully designed temple doors.

Along
guide

FREIBERG GERMANY TEMPLE

DEDICATED 1985

The Freiberg Germany Temple was the only temple built and dedicated in a communist-controlled country (the German Democratic Republic, commonly known as East Germany), the result of many significant miracles. Some fifteen years after it opened, it was remodeled to nearly double its original size. At that time, a statue of the Angel Moroni was placed atop the temple tower. At the time of its rededication in 2002, the temple served members in Germany, Poland, the Czech Republic, Hungary, Bulgaria, Romania, and the Ukraine. (See page 142 for additional background on this temple.)

The Brandenburg Gate in Berlin.

Sunrise over a coal mine shaft as seen from the temple. Freiberg is famous for its coal mines.

ABOVE: *What is left of the infamous Berlin Wall.*
BELOW LEFT: *"Checkpoint Charlie," a guardhouse on the Berlin Wall.* BELOW RIGHT: *Stake center in Berlin; note the missionaries on the left.*

ABOVE LEFT: *The door of the Wittenberg chapel, near Freiberg, where Martin Luther nailed his famous "ninety-five theses," a key event in the Protestant Reformation.*
BELOW: *The Potsdam Bridge in Berlin.*

DEDICATED 1972

The community surrounding the Provo Utah Temple has long been of vital importance to the Church; it includes the huge campus of Brigham Young University and the Missionary Training Center. When the temple was dedicated, the two dedicatory sessions were broadcast to the 23,000-seat Marriott Center on the BYU campus nearby.

The Provo Utah Temple is said to be the busiest in the Church. It stands proudly topped with a new Angel Moroni statue placed there in 2003.

The mountain of the house of the Lord shall be established in the top of the mountains, . . . and people shall flow unto it. And many nations shall come, and say, Come, and let us go up to the mountain of the Lord, and to the house of the God of Jacob.

—MICAH 4: 1–2

DEDICATED 2000

The first baptisms in New Mexico occurred in the 1870s, when two missionaries baptized more than a hundred Zuni Indians in the Little Colorado River. Since then the Church in New Mexico has grown to some 60,000 members. The Albuquerque New Mexico Temple also serves members in parts of Arizona and Colorado.

The view from the west of the temple is completely different from that of the east. The west side (above) has the main entrance and parking lot; the east side (right) is close to the street.

FAR LEFT AND BELOW LEFT: *Scenes from the Annual Albuquerque Hot Air Balloon Festival, which draws balloonists and spectators from all over the United States and beyond.*
RIGHT: *The rugged, haunting quality of mountain views typical in this Southwest region.*

DEDICATED 1974

The seven images of this magnificent temple are intermingled with monuments for freedom in our nation's capital, which freedom was part of God's plan. The monuments are the Lincoln Memorial, the Jefferson Memorial, the Capitol of the United States, the Washington Monument, the World War II Iwo Jima sculpture, and the Arlington National Cemetery. The temple and these monuments seem to join in their witness that America is a nation established through the power of God—and that we must remain righteous to remain free.

LEFT: *Motorists on Interstate 495 are treated to the stunning view of the needle-like spires towering above them.*

ABOVE: *The spires produce an interesting visual phenomenon: they change in color and density from light gold to dark gold and from dark gold to pitch-black according to the light and time of day.*

ABOVE: *The Jefferson Memorial.*
BELOW LEFT: *The Lincoln Memorial.*

Arlington National Cemetery.

Except the Lord build the house, they labour in vain that build it.
—PSALM 127:1

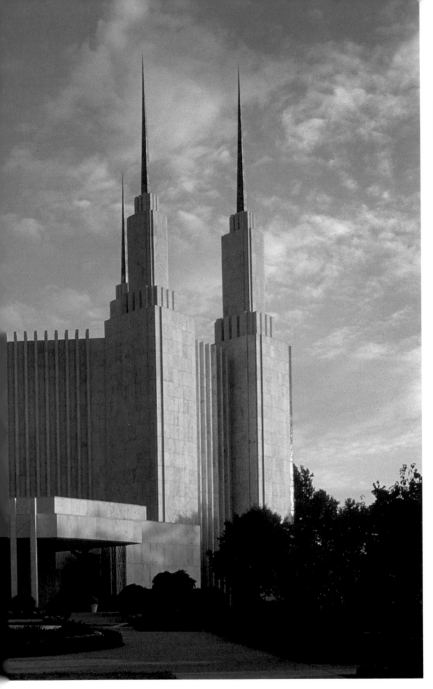

ABOVE: *The Washington Monument.*
BELOW RIGHT: *The United States Marine Memorial,*
also known as the Iwo Jima Memorial.

BELOW: *The Capitol building of the United States of America.*

DEDICATED 1999

To get to Colonia Juárez we first had to endure a lengthy border crossing, followed by a half-day drive. I had the feeling we were going to a very isolated countryside, which indeed we were. The paved road literally stops in Colonia Juárez, with dirt roads continuing to farms.

This area was settled by Mormons in the 1880s. At present there are some 5,000 Latter-day Saints who are served by this small temple.

BELOW: *The sun catches the hills above the temple and little town.*

At night, the temple lights leave no mistake about the presence of this beacon in this historic community.

MONTRÉAL QUÉBEC TEMPLE

DEDICATED 2000

After a long drive from Boston, carefully following directions and maps, we found ourselves lost in Montréal. There were many friendly people willing to give us directions, but not many who could understand our English. We realized we were in French-speaking Québec and not upper New Hampshire or Vermont. Finally I spotted the temple from the highway and was eventually able to take an exit and find it.

Like so many times on this temple photography project, we found that though the journey was daunting and sometimes intimidating, the destination was very sweet. A beautiful temple greeted us, with a friendly familiarity, and we were happy to stay close to it until our mission of attendance and photo coverage was accomplished.

This temple is bilingual: ordinances are conducted in French and English.

ABOVE: *Panorama of the Montréal skyline as viewed from across the St. Lawrence River.*

LEFT: *The stadium for the Montréal Olympics of 1976.*

DEDICATED 1998

The Preston England Temple is displayed on a lovely landscaped hill and can be seen from the major road that junctions nearby. The temple is part of a large campus that includes a missionary training center and stake center, all tied together but segregated by lovely and inviting landscaping. The overall effect creates a place you delight to arrive at and wish not to leave.

This temple is built at a location of extreme importance to Latter-day Saints. In this area in 1837 and 1838, LDS missionaries baptized more than 2,000 converts, many of whom later immigrated to the United States and became a strong part of the early Church.

ABOVE: *A side view gives a sense of the large scale of this building.*
BELOW: *The white granite blocks shimmer in the first rays of the morning sun.*

ABOVE: *A fish-eye view of the night-lighted temple and reflecting pools.*
BELOW: *The River Ribble, where the first baptisms in England took place.*

The exterior walkway displays temple symbols carved in stone.

LEFT, ABOVE, AND BELOW: *Scenes from Albert Dock in Liverpool, which was a major emigration departure center for the early Saints.*

ABOVE: *The Missionary Training Center in Preston is located near the temple grounds.*
LEFT: *The obelisk in Preston's Market Place was erected in 1782; it was restored in 1979.*

The lights in the tower give a lovely lamp or lighthouse effect that seems very appropriate in the Lancashire area.

DEDICATED 2001

Located in southeastern Washington, this temple captured me with the elegance of its architecture. I particularly enjoyed the welcoming porch.

The Church was first organized in this area in 1944. Early congregations met in a doctor's office, a fire station, a grange hall, and an old radio building. Now there are eleven stakes and 34,000 members in the area.

ABOVE AND BELOW: *Mt. Hood and the Columbia River are delightful features of the landscape of this region.*

The temple stands close by the stake center in this panoramic view.

FRESNO CALIFORNIA TEMPLE

ABOVE: *A tree-lined street in a well-planned residential area leads to the temple.*
BELOW: *Olive trees in front of the temple bring to mind the importance of olive trees and olive oil in gospel symbolism.*

DEDICATED 2000

California has more members of the Church than any other state besides Utah. Accordingly, it has more temples than any other state besides Utah. California has five functioning temples, with two others under construction; Utah has eleven temples.

The Fresno California Temple, one of the smaller temples built under the direction of President Gordon B. Hinckley, took just one year to construct.

ABOVE: *The same granite was used in the construction of the Fresno California Temple as was used in the Oakland California Temple 200 miles away, which for years served Latter-day Saints from the Fresno area.*

BELOW: *Grapevines and grapes indicate the importance of agriculture to people in this fertile area.*

DEDICATED 1985

The first missionaries arrived in Korea in 1954. In the few decades since, the Church in South Korea has grown to more than 70,000 members in seventeen stakes. This temple is the first built on mainland Asia.

The temple garden fits with and frames this appropriate temple design. Space is precious in this highly populated country and is used with wisdom.

All Korea photographs by Drake Busath.

The Korean flag waves near the temple spire.

Trees in a park form a lovely design.

Busy street scene near the temple.

말일성도 예수 그리스도 교회
한국 서울 성전
SEOUL KOREA TEMPLE
THE CHURCH OF JESUS CHRIST OF LATTER-DAY SAINTS

Temple entrance sign.

ABOVE: *Squid in fish market.*
BELOW: *Market display.*
BELOW LEFT: *Mask from nearby island culture.*

DENVER COLORADO TEMPLE

DEDICATED 1986

Shown here in five variations of light and color, the spire of the Denver temple stands as a herald to the people in eastern Colorado. The temple lot is surrounded by an attractive residential neighborhood in Littleton, south of downtown Denver. West from Denver, the freeway travels through major ski areas, through Grand Junction, and then to eastern Utah.

BELOW: *The Colorado National Monument offers a breathtaking view.*

DEDICATED 2002

Brazil is one of the wonders of Church growth in our day. In 1957 the Church had only a thousand members there. Now it has more than a thousand *wards*. In total, the Church in Brazil has more than 800,000 members in 183 stakes.

The Campinas Brazil Temple is one of four temples in Brazil (with a fifth temple announced). Campinas, a city of 2 million people, is located eighty miles west of São Paulo, Brazil's largest city (with 18 million people).

BELOW: *Even walkways and sidewalks are colorful in Brazil. The waving design in this sidewalk is repeated around the city. This walk is next to an LDS ward we attended.* RIGHT: *The warm colors in the stone slabs leading to the decorative design around the fountain are enhanced in the dusk light by the falling rain.*

ABOVE: *The temple marble gleams in the morning light.* BELOW LEFT: *The temple overlooks the city.* BELOW RIGHT: *Olympic gold medal winner Tara Lipinski teaches a young student in an ice rink located in a large, upscale mall.*

The Copacabana Beach at Rio de Janeiro.

The temple on the hill is back lit against the early morning sunrise.

New parents nuzzling their tender offspring.

I will make . . . an everlasting covenant with them: and I will . . . set my sanctuary in the midst of them for evermore.
—EZEKIEL 37:26

Early morning sun warms the temple. Note the high arched porticos on each side.

ABOVE: *The royal poinciana tree, seen all around Campinas, arches above a street fair.*

ABOVE: *The lighted fountain frames a wedding party at the temple entrance.*
LEFT: *An artist displays his work at a fair. Note the McDonald's Restaurant across the street next to red Spanish architecture.*

BELOW: *Lake Powell, a huge reservoir that provides water and recreation for millions.*

DEDICATED 1998

This lovely temple was the first of the smaller temples. It is expertly crafted of the finest materials and workmanship. Extra marble was imported and enhances the look of the temple. The Monticello Utah Temple was greatly expanded and rededicated in 2002.

The San Juan–Monticello area is in the center of some of the most spectacular and well-known red-rock country in the world. This area was first settled by Latter-day Saints in the 1870s.

Monticello is located in the Four Corners area, where the borders of four states come together: Utah, Colorado, New Mexico, and Arizona.

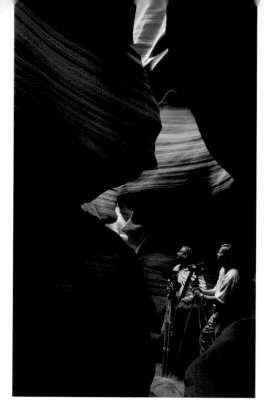

ABOVE AND FAR RIGHT: *Mesa Verde National Park Indian ruins.*
RIGHT: *Slot canyon near Page, Arizona, and the Lake Powell dam.*
BELOW: *Arches National Park, a wonderland of natural arches and huge slabs of red sandstone of many shapes.*

Monument Valley, located on the border of Utah and Arizona.

ABOVE AND BELOW: *Mesa Verde, in southwestern Colorado.*

This country has haunting qualities that are calming to my soul. Our family hosted a group of master photographers from around the United States and several other countries. They came to Salt Lake City, heard a Mormon Tabernacle Choir broadcast, then traveled to Moab for several days to visit Arches National Park. Everybody loved it—but at one point in Arches, I noticed a portrait photographer from San Francisco sitting on a rock with his head down. Worried, I asked if he was okay. He looked up and said, "Don, I have never been in a place I have enjoyed more. I will return here often. The peace and tranquillity is marvelous."

These natural attractions are so popular to visitors worldwide that it is not uncommon to hear several languages in the same cafe.

ABOVE: *Monticello Utah Temple after a snowstorm.* BELOW LEFT: *Shiprock Peak, in northwestern New Mexico.* BELOW RIGHT: *Moon from Dead Horse Point.*

DEDICATED 2002

This was the first of Europe's smaller temples to be completed. It is in the suburb of The Hague called Zoetermeer, which translates literally to "sweet lake."

The Hague Netherlands Temple serves five stakes in the Netherlands and Belgium. The forerunner to one of those stakes, the Holland Stake, was the first non-English–language stake established in the Church; formed in 1961, the Holland Stake was created exactly one hundred years after the first baptism in the country.

ABOVE: *Tulip farm fields so typical in spring.*
BELOW: *Canals and water management are essential to the making and preservation of the Netherlands, so it is appropriate that the temple stands next to a beautiful canal running through Zoetermeer.*

ABOVE: *A fish-eye lens allows us to see the reflecting pool with a walking bridge at the temple entrance.*
BELOW: *Classic architecture in the Netherlands. Note the stork poised on its nest.*

ON THESE PAGES: *When the world thinks of Holland, they think of flowers, windmills, and canals. We enjoyed all those in abundance, as shown in these photographs. The Keukenhof Gardens, the far-right photo, are a must see!*

The Lord is in his holy temple.
—PSALM 11:4

DEDICATED 2002

Snowflake, Arizona, was settled by William J. Flake in the 1870s under the direction of Elder Erastus Snow (a member of the Council of the Twelve) and other Church leaders. The first of thirty-four such settlements in Arizona, it was also the location of the first stake there.

When Donna and I drove to Snowflake we were impressed to find an upscale community seemingly "out in the middle of nowhere." We were further amazed to find this beautiful new temple on a hill, unique not only in location, but in design. Notice the dark stone at the base. Like many temples, water is featured near the entryway.

ABOVE: *Desert landscaping is tastefully used along the entrance road.*
LEFT: *This monument depicts Erastus Snow meeting with the William J. Flake family, who had discovered and settled this area—hence the name Snowflake.*
BELOW: *A golf course meanders around the base of the temple hill.*

DEDICATED 1993

As we talked to many people and shared plans for this collection of temples, we were often asked, "Have you photographed the San Diego Temple yet?" No, we hadn't. The follow-up comment invariably was, "You *have* to include that one."

I, of course, had seen photos of the temple before we finally arrived there in 2003—but that didn't diminish my first visual encounter with the building in person. Because of the high interest in this building, we had allowed three full days and nights. I needed every minute. Dating back to my training in architectural photography with Hal Rumel in the late fifties, I usually follow the practice of circling a building to study it from every available angle, observing lighting possibilities during different times of day and night and noting what special equipment and film might be needed. The temple was so fascinating; it was hard to pull myself away from the temple to get photos of other parts of San Diego, which were plentiful.

It is apparent to me that the architect used light to the fullest extent possible. The sharp angles of the spires, combined with the windows of decorative glass used throughout (including high in the spires), make possible a different look with each movement of the sun—or lack of sun—and into the night.

The San Diego California Temple is spectacular inside as well as outside. I have felt blessed that photographs are not allowed inside the temples, because I can go inside with Donna and be assured in every temple that the experience will be familiar, consistent, restful, uplifting, and productive of the peace that comes with unselfish service. Think of that—it's been the same in every temple we have attended! Inside each temple, of course, the décor and furnishings are unique and quite individual.

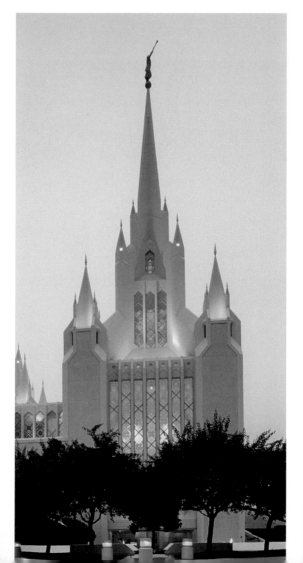

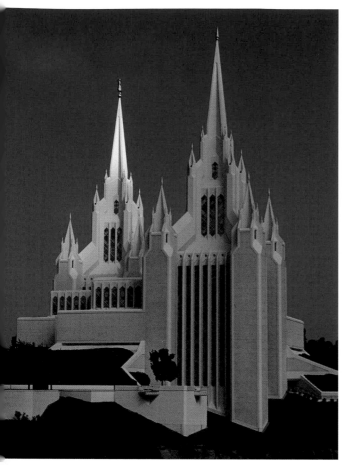

ABOVE LEFT: *The phenomenon of seeing only one spire lighted certainly quickened my pulse! This view is from across the freeway.* ABOVE RIGHT: *The Spanish-style buildings at San Diego's Balboa Park contrast with a busy airport.* BELOW RIGHT: *Lily pads at Balboa Park.*

ABOVE AND RIGHT: *The spires of this temple show translucency, reflectivity, and only the delicate suggestion of shape and light when shrouded with fog. Each view is inspiring.*

And thou shalt make holy garments for Aaron thy brother for glory and for beauty.
—EXODUS 28:2

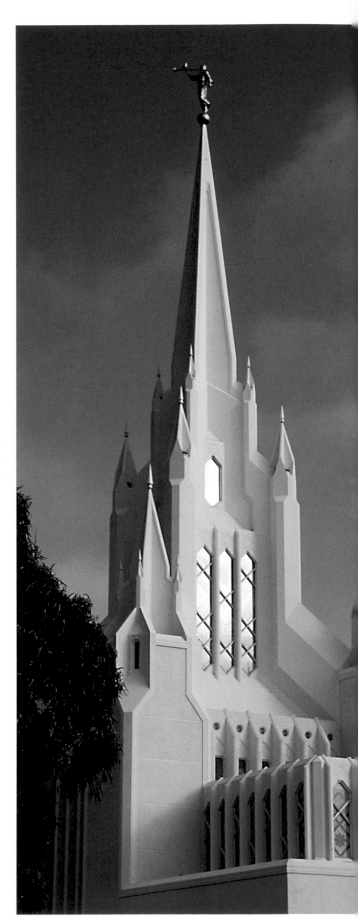

DEDICATED 2003

The newest temple in this collection is the Redlands California Temple, located in the heart of orange-grove country. In fact, the temple itself is built on the site of what was once an orange grove. The finishing work on construction was proceeding while we were there.

Redlands is only ten miles from San Bernardino, California, which was settled by Mormons in 1851. The land on which the Redlands temple is located was part of the Saints' original purchase of 35,000 acres for $77,500.

BELOW: *Beyond the oranges, the statue of the angel Moroni can be seen across the street.*

The temple stands near the existing stake center.

*The design and the detail of the spire tower
are simple yet striking.*

DEDICATED 2000

This temple of gleaming white Mexican marble serves members from both sides of the border—from El Paso, Texas, and Ciudad, Mexico. Church leaders placed the temple on the Mexico side because it is easier for patrons to travel south from the United States than go north from Mexico. The temple is located thirty miles south of the border.

Both Mexican and American Saints were heavily involved in constructing this temple; it is estimated that members donated more than 50,000 hours of labor on the temple.

Two flags mark the border between Mexico and the United States.

DEDICATED 1984

In 1939, Ezra Taft Benson, the stake president in Boise, Idaho, invited President Heber J. Grant to visit Boise to look at available temple sites. The area was considered, but Church leaders eventually decided to build a temple in eastern Idaho at Idaho Falls instead. Forty-five years later, the Boise Idaho Temple became a reality. The Boise temple serves thirty-three stakes in western Idaho and three in eastern Oregon.

On visiting this temple, I enjoyed the textured look of the stone work and the six-spire design.

A typical Idaho hay field under a dramatic gathering storm.

The west side of the temple has the entryway and parking.

The Sawtooth Mountains near Ketchum, Idaho, and the Sun Valley resort.

DEDICATED 1996

Nestled against the majestic mountains, this temple fits its name well. The blue-green glass in the spire makes a lovely complement to the hills behind, reminding me of the glacier-melt pool found on the back side of Mt. Timpanogos. This temple building can be seen for miles from the main highway and is a beacon at night.

The Mount Timpanogos Utah Temple serves fifty-three stakes, primarily in northern Utah County.

DEDICATED 1995

In some ways, the Bountiful Utah Temple is a twin of the Mount Timpanogos Utah Temple. They were constructed only a year and a half apart. The two temples are identical in size and dimension (although the spire on the Mount Timpanogos Utah Temple is 14 feet taller, rising to 190 feet). And they serve as bookends to the Salt Lake Valley, Bountiful to the north and Mount Timpanogos to the south.

LAS VEGAS NEVADA TEMPLE

DEDICATED 1989

Avisitor from Minnesota to the Las Vegas Nevada Temple open house (one of nearly 300,000) was quoted by Chad Hawkins, in *The First 100 Temples*, as saying, "This is one of the most beautiful houses of worship I have ever attended."

I can certainly echo that statement. As we went to visit this temple soon after it was dedicated, we had no preconceived notions. I was very pleasantly surprised. It is a distinctive and individual building. The interior continues the drama of the exterior in a very tasteful way. This temple stands in holy contrast to the worldliness found in some other areas of the city.

DEDICATED 2000

The Boston Massachusetts Temple was the one-hundredth temple of The Church of Jesus Christ of Latter-day Saints, and it was dedicated in the year 2000. The dedication came only after many challenges, but the Lord's plan and program prevailed.

The Boston area is important to Church history. Several early leaders of the Church preached the restored gospel there, including Joseph Smith, Brigham Young, and Wilford Woodruff. Two branches of the Church were established in Boston in 1832.

The Boston Massachusetts Temple serves members in Connecticut, Maine, Massachusetts, New Hampshire, parts of New York, and Rhode Island.

LEFT: *The entry marker.* BELOW: *Boatmen training for a regatta, which was held the following day. The Boston skyline is enhanced by rich fall colors.*

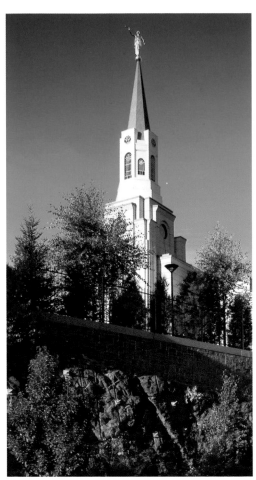

ABOVE LEFT: *The Minuteman Statue, honoring the early defenders of America's freedom, located a few minutes' drive from Temple Hill.* BELOW: *The expression "a house built upon a rock" is literally true for the Boston Massachusetts Temple.*

ABOVE, ABOVE RIGHT, AND BELOW: *Three lovely harbor scenes, typical of the area.*

The pathway to the temple from the parking lot.

The lane leading to Sharon, Vermont, birthplace of Joseph Smith. Sharon is 140 miles from Boston.

A boatslip in Rockport, 40 miles north of Boston.

ABOVE: *A New England scene, with the South Royalton Ward meetinghouse (in Sharon, Vermont) in the background.*
BELOW: *A typical New England home, patriotically displaying the flag.*

The Joseph Smith birthplace marker at Sharon, Vermont.

TOKYO JAPAN TEMPLE

DEDICATED 1980

When President Spencer W. Kimball announced in the Tokyo Area Conference in 1975 that a temple was planned for Japan, the congregation burst into spontaneous applause—and then burst into tears. The Tokyo Japan Temple was the first built in Asia. It serves twenty-six stakes, fourteen districts in Japan. (A smaller temple, the Fukuoka Japan Temple, serves an additional four stakes and five districts.)

The temple and its spire rise vertically in a quiet neighborhood in one of the most densely populated cities in the world (33 million people in the metropolitan area; 33,000 persons per square mile in the city itself). The grounds of the temple are small, but very serene.

All Japan photographs by Drake Busath.

ABOVE: *A beautiful public pool, with the temple in the background.*
LEFT: *Close-up of temple gardens, with a replica of a traditional Japanese urn.*

ABOVE: *The entry marker.*
BELOW: *A street scene near the temple, showing a very crowded neighborhood!*

ACCRA GHANA TEMPLE

DEDICATED 2004

In early 1978, the Church had no official presence at all in West Africa. Now there are twenty-two stakes and eighteen districts in the Accra Ghana Temple district. Countries represented in this district are Ghana, Nigeria, Liberia, Ivory Coast, and Sierra Leone. Total membership in these nations adds up to about 150,000 people.

Did we experience any surprises on our arrival in Ghana? Several:

- the modesty of the men and women;
- the spiritual overtones of the city and the spiritual maturity of the Saints;
- the happiness and kindness of everyone;
- the beauty of the landscape;
- the color-rich clothing.

I have tried to capture the feeling of these things in the photographs on these pages.

Tree and impressive termite mound.

Saints gathering in the meetinghouse adjacent to the temple.

Foliage on temple grounds.

The beautiful architecture and design of the temple grounds.

ON THESE PAGES: *Representative scenes from the beautiful people and land of Ghana, Africa.*

Background on the Freiberg Germany Temple

Every temple has a story behind it—a story of the temple itself as well as of its people. As one example, here is a brief summary of the background of the Freiberg Germany Temple.

The first East German Latter-day Saint to be called as patriarch in the German Democratic Republic was Walter Krause, who briefly described the first patriarchal blessing he ever gave. A woman had made an appointment to meet Brother Krause in Dresden to receive her blessing. When the day came, Brother Krause felt unprepared to give the blessing. He nearly sent the woman home. Instead, he sent her on a short walk, giving himself additional time to access the Lord's Spirit. After receiving the distinct impression that he should simply begin, Brother Krause gave the woman a blessing in which he said that she would be able to fulfill her long-time wish of attending the House of the Lord.

Two years later, Brother Krause was attending a conference in Schwerin and heard that this sister was at home with a serious sickness. He visited her and she reminded him that he had promised her she would go to the temple. She recovered from her illness, and in 1985, as the Freiberg Germany Temple was dedicated, this sister stood on the front steps waiting for Patriarch Krause, to whom she said, "Mit meinem Patrarchen, zur Besichtigung des Tempels, will ich den Tempel betreten" [With my patriarch, at the visit to the temple, I would like to enter the temple] (Krause Oral History, LDS Church Archives, 57).

For years, East German Latter-day Saints had petitioned the communist government for permission to travel to Switzerland to attend the temple. Countless times these requests were denied. In April 1975, Elder Thomas S. Monson, then of the Quorum of the Twelve Apostles with a special assignment to minister to the Saints in East Germany, was in the German Democratic Republic. There he offered a prayer in behalf of the Church members and the entire country in which he asked, "Heavenly Father, wilt Thou open up the way that the faithful may be accorded the privilege of going to Thy holy temple, there to receive their holy endowments and to be sealed as families for time and all eternity. . . .

"[And] wilt Thou intervene in the governmental affairs. Cause that Thy Holy Spirit may dwell with those who preside, that their hearts may be touched and that they may make those decisions which would help in the advancement of Thy work" (Thomas S. Monson, *Faith Rewarded: A Personal Account of Prophetic Promises to the East German Saints* [Salt Lake City: Deseret Book, 1996], 36).

The Freiberg Germany Temple was dedicated on June 20–30, 1985, by President Gordon B. Hinckley. In his prayer, President Hinckley expressed gratitude to "the officers of the government who have given encouragement and made available land and materials."

He concluded the dedicatory prayer by saying, "May this day long be remembered in the annals of Thy Church. May it be recalled with gratitude and appreciation. May it mark the beginning of a new day of gladness for Thy people. May their tears turn to smiles. May their burdens be lightened. May their cares lifted. May the assurance that Thou art near strengthen every heart.

"Thou knowest we have long prayed that we might have a temple in our midst" (Gordon B. Hinckley, dedicatory prayer, June 20, 1985).

The Freiberg Germany Temple was rededicated September 7, 2002, by President Hinckley. "Seventeen years ago we dedicated the original structure," he said during the prayer. "It was built under remarkable circumstances and has well served Thy faithful sons and daughters. Since then, marvelous and wonderful happenings have occurred in this land. The nation of Germany, once divided, has become one. The infamous wall is gone, and the people of the land mingle freely together.

"We thank Thee for the manifestation of Thy power when this temple was first built, that Thou didst touch the hearts of men in a miraculous manner to make it possible to construct it and dedicate it to the blessing of the very many who have used it" (Gordon B. Hinckley, rededication prayer, September 7, 2002).

The Freiberg Germany Temple stands as a testimony to the dedication of the East German Latter-day Saints, who endured over forty years of isolation and subtle oppression. Concerning this, President Thomas S. Monson wrote, "People will ask, 'How has it been possible for the Church to obtain permission to build a temple behind the Iron Curtain?' My feeling is simply that the faith and devotion of our Latter-day Saints in that area brought forth the help of Almighty God. . . . All honor and glory belong to our Heavenly Father, for it is only through His divine intervention that these events have taken place" (Monson, *Faith Rewarded*, 105–6).

—Matthew Heiss